The GALAXY GUIDES

ARE THERE OTHER GALAXIES?

Alix Wood

PowerKiDS press

Published in 2016 by **Rosen Publishing**
29 East 21st Street, New York, NY 10010

Copyright © 2016 Alix Wood Books

Editor: Eloise Macgregor
Designer: Alix Wood
Consultant: Kevin E. Yates, Fellow of the Royal Astronomical Society

Photo Credits: Cover, 1, 4-5, 5 bottom, 7 top, 9 main image, 12, 14 bottom, 15 middle, 16-17, 20, 21 top and middle, 22-23 © NASA; 5 top inset © NASA/ESA/M J Jee/ H Ford; 6, 8, 15 top, 17, 19 top, 23 inset, 24, 25, 26, 27 © Dollar Photo Club; 9 top © Wally Pacholka; 10 © NASA/J Blakeslee; 11 bottom © NASA/ESA/Hubble Heritage Team; 13 top © John P Gleason; 13 bottom © Space Art; 14 middle © NASA/R Ibata; 15 bottom © Alix Wood; 18 © NASA/Debra Meloy Elmegreen; 19 bottom © NASA/ESA/Z Levay/R van der Marel/STscI/T Hallas/A Mellinger; 21 bottom © Alix Wood

Cataloging-in-Publication Data

Wood, Alix.
Are there other galaxies? / by Alix Wood.
p. cm. — (The galaxy guides)
Includes index.
ISBN 978-1-4994-0875-1 (pbk.)
ISBN 978-1-4994-0870-6 (6 pack)
ISBN 978-1-4994-0869-0 (library binding)
1. Galaxies — Juvenile literature. I. Wood, Alix. II. Title.
QB857.3 W66 2016
523.1'12—d23

Manufactured in the United States of America

CPSIA Compliance Information: Batch #: WS15PK
For Further Information contact Rosen Publishing, New York, New York at 1-800-237-9932

Contents

What Is a Galaxy?

A galaxy is a large group of stars, gas, and dust held together by **gravity**. There are billions of galaxies in the **Universe**. Galaxies with less than a billion stars are small galaxies. In our galaxy the Sun is just one of between 100 and 400 billion stars! It's very hard to accurately say how many stars a galaxy has. Scientists base their estimate on the galaxy's size.

Scientists think that there are several billion galaxies in the Universe. The exact number is not known. Scientists counted how many galaxies they could see in a small area of the sky. From this number they estimated how many galaxies there might be in the entire sky. Some, called **dwarf galaxies**, are very small with about 10 million stars. Some of the largest galaxies are thought to have 100 trillion stars.

The word galaxy comes from the Greek word "galaxias" which means "milky." Earth's galaxy (pictured) is called the Milky Way. It does look a little like a band of milky light across the sky.

Gravity and Dark Matter

Scientists believe that most of the mass of a galaxy is made up of a mysterious substance known as "dark matter." The theory is hard to prove, as dark matter is invisible! The only way you can tell it is there is by the effect its gravity has on matter that we can see. Gravity is the force that causes objects to move toward each other. The more **mass** an object has, the more gravity it has.

Dark matter is invisible. In this photo color has been added so you can see the dark matter as a ring of dark blue pulling the paler blue matter toward it.

There are different types of galaxies. They are grouped based on their shape. Some galaxies are shaped like **spirals**. Others are shaped like **ellipses**. Some have no distinct shape. The famous scientist Edwin Hubble invented this system of groups. He discovered a lot about galaxies. The Hubble Space **Telescope** is named after him.

Hubble Space Telescope

How Were Galaxies Formed?

Scientists believe galaxies were formed after an explosion, known as the "Big Bang." This explosion created clouds of gases that became the galaxies' building blocks.

One piece of evidence that shows the Big Bang happened is a faint glow in space. Telescopes in space can see a patchy pattern of slightly warmer and cooler gas all around us.

How Can an Explosion Produce a Galaxy?

The dense areas in space pulled in any material around them because they had more gravity. The gas became hot and dense enough for the first stars to form. Some scientists believe that clusters of stars formed first, which later gathered into galaxies. Others believe that galaxies formed first and the stars within them gathered into clusters later.

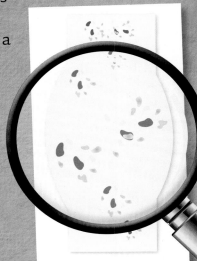

A photograph from the Hubble Space Telescope of the distant Swan Nebula, showing newly born stars and surrounding gas.

HANDS-ON SCIENCE

Can You Prove There Is Matter Everywhere?

You will need: clear tape, white paper, magnifying glass

Go on a dust hunt. Take a strip of sticky tape and find a dusty area. The tops of doors or under furniture are good places. Press the tape lightly onto the area and then lift it up again. Stick your tape onto some white paper. Look through a magnifying glass and you will probably find all kinds of different dust.

How can galaxies form from tiny dust? Gravity pulls the matter together and spins it slowly. Some of the matter becomes hot and forms stars. Surrounding matter turns into discs which eventually form planets!

There are three kinds of galaxies: spiral, elliptical, and **irregular**. The only difference between the three is what shape they are. Our galaxy is a type of spiral galaxy.

The spiral arms in this kind of galaxy are like circling waves. These waves cause new stars to form. Some of the new stars created in the wave are very large. These large stars glow brightly, causing the nearby dust clouds to glow. The large bright stars don't live very long. Their large size means that they burn all their fuel very quickly. Usually they die before they leave the wave. Only the smaller, dimmer stars survive to leave the waves they formed in.

HANDS-ON SCIENCE

Create Your Own Spiral Galaxy!

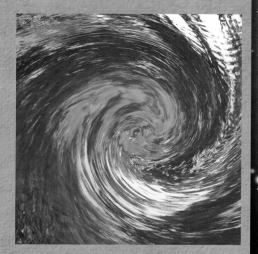

You will need: a large glass jar or jug, paper, a hole punch, a wooden spoon, some water

Half fill the jar with water. Punch fifty or so holes from the paper using the hole punch. The holes will be stars and planets in your galaxy. You could draw on them, if you like. Sprinkle the holes into the water. With the handle of your wooden spoon, stir the water in the jar around in a circle. Keep stirring until the water creates a spiral. Remove the spoon and watch your galaxy!

The Milky Way is known as a barrel spiral galaxy. This is because it has a long bar shape in the middle with spiral arms coming off the ends. Spiral galaxies are believed to be younger than elliptical galaxies. As spiral galaxies burn through their gas and stop producing stars they lose their spiral shape and slowly turn into elliptical galaxies.

An artist's drawing of the Milky Way.

The Milky Way has two major arms, filled with young and old stars. The other minor arms are mainly filled with gas and star-forming activity.

What Do Other Types of Galaxies Look Like?

Elliptical galaxies are a mass of stars formed into an ellipse-shaped disc. Galaxies that have no obvious spiral or ellipse shape are known as irregular galaxies. It is thought that most irregular galaxies were formed by two or more galaxies merging into each other!

The giant elliptical galaxy ESO 325-G004. Not all galaxies have names too, some are just known by letters and numbers.

Elliptical galaxies don't create many new stars, so the stars in them are mostly very old. The stars are very close together, making the center look like one big star. If Earth was in an elliptical galaxy, it would be light night and day!

How Can You Tell How Old a Star Is?

A star cluster showing their different colors. The red stars are near the end of their lives.

Stars vary in size, color, and brightness. They can be red, orange, yellow, white, or blue. Scientists can look at the color of a star and tell how hot it is. A star turns different colors when it is at different stages, and when it is at different temperatures. Stars spend most of their lives burning the **hydrogen** gas in their **core**. The length of time they spend doing this depends on their mass. Burning hydrogen produces **helium** gas. When a star has used up all its hydrogen, it burns the helium instead.

Around a quarter of all galaxies are irregular galaxies. Irregular galaxies can be any shape. Many irregular galaxies may have been spiral or elliptical until they had some kind of event which altered them, such as crashing into another galaxy. They are often an odd shape because they are influenced by the gravity of other galaxies close by.

What Is Earth's Galaxy Like?

The Milky Way contains between 100 and 400 billion stars, and a similar number of planets. One of the stars is our Sun. Our Sun lies near a small, partial arm called the Orion Spur, between the Sagittarius and Perseus arms. Earth is a very, very tiny part of the galaxy.

Size comparison of the Sun and the planets

Sun

Earth

Scientists using space telescopes have been able to figure out the shape of our galaxy. There are two main arms which spiral out from either end of a central bar of stars. Other smaller arms spiral from the center, too. The center of the Milky Way contains a **black hole**. A black hole sucks in any matter that gets close to it, a little like an enormous vacuum cleaner.

FACT FILE

Do We Move Around the Center of the Milky Way?

When an object moves around another object it is called an **orbit**. Our Sun orbits the center of the Milky Way, and as we orbit the Sun, it takes us along for the ride. It takes between 225 million and 250 million years for the Sun to complete its orbit! The time it takes for one orbit is known as a Galactic Year. It takes a long time because the Sun is around 27,000 light-years from the center of the galaxy. That's a long way. A light-year is the distance traveled by a beam of light in one year. A light-year is around 6 trillion (6,000,000,000,000) miles or 10 trillion (10,000,000,000,000) km!

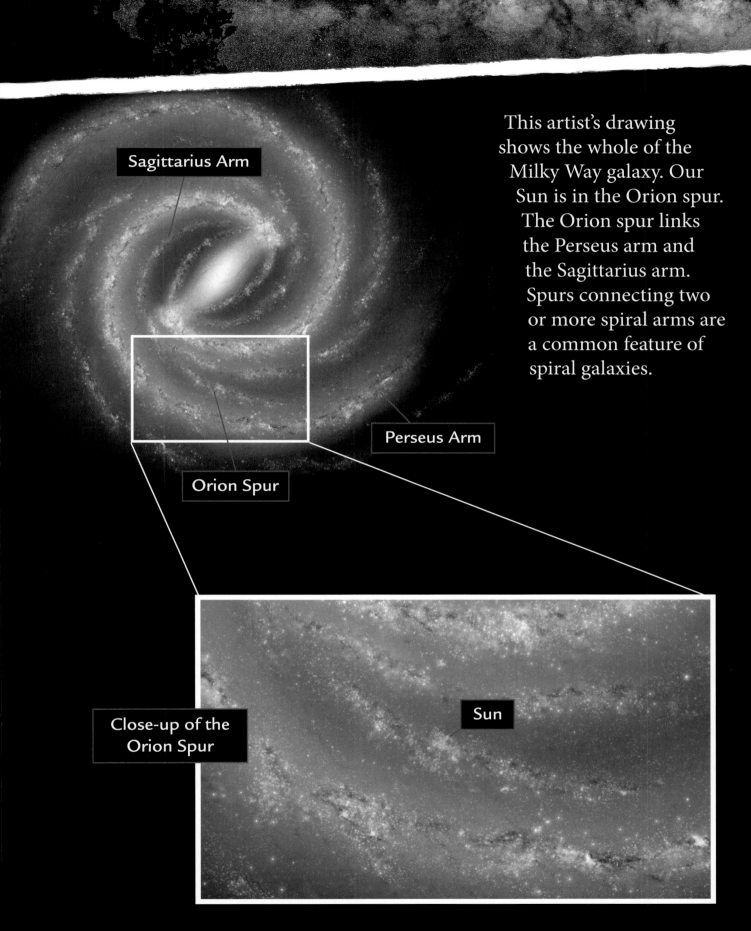

Sagittarius Arm

This artist's drawing shows the whole of the Milky Way galaxy. Our Sun is in the Orion spur. The Orion spur links the Perseus arm and the Sagittarius arm. Spurs connecting two or more spiral arms are a common feature of spiral galaxies.

Perseus Arm

Orion Spur

Close-up of the Orion Spur

Sun

Are There Any Other Galaxies Close to Us?

The term "close" is not really very accurate! There are some other galaxies near ours, but they are a very long way away. Our Milky Way galaxy is part of a group of galaxies known as "The Local Group." There are around 54 galaxies in the Local Group. The largest galaxies in the group are the Andromeda Galaxy, the Milky Way, and Triangulum.

Sun

Canis Major Dwarf

Canis Major Dwarf is believed to be our closest galaxy. It is actually within the Milky Way itself. It is an irregular galaxy around 25,000 light-years away from the Sun. Some scientists don't think it is a real galaxy, but just part of the Milky Way.

Triangulum is the third largest spiral galaxy in the Local Group. It is also known as the Pinwheel Galaxy. Scientists believe Triangulum measures about 50,000 light-years across. That's half the **diameter** of the Milky Way.

Andromeda is our closest spiral galaxy, and the largest galaxy in the Local Group. It is over 2 million light-years away. It is estimated to be about 160,000 light-years in diameter and contains more than 2 trillion stars! The galaxy is so big it can be seen with the naked eye on moonless nights. Only the bright center is visible unless you use a powerful telescope.

HANDS-ON SCIENCE

Make Your Own Galaxy in a Bottle

You will need: a plastic bottle, baby oil, water, fine glitter, red and blue food coloring, an old bowl, old clothes

Wear some old clothes. Mix the water and food coloring together in the bowl until you get a good dark purple color. Half fill the bottle with baby oil. Add the colored water and a handful of glitter. Put on the lid and swirl the bottle around. The more you shake and turn the bottle, the more it will look like the night sky. Bubbles should appear and start to sparkle like the stars!

Earth orbits around the Sun, and the Sun orbits around the center of the Milky Way. At the same time, the Milky Way and other galaxies are moving, too. Groups of galaxies, known as clusters, rotate around the center of mass of the cluster. Galaxies are also moving away from each other because the Universe is still expanding after the Big Bang.

FACT FILE

Hubble and the Expanding Galaxy

In 1925, **astronomer** Edwin Hubble first discovered that galaxies other than the Milky Way existed. Hubble also discovered that the Universe is expanding by watching the speed that galaxies moved apart. Scientists now use light from exploded stars to measure a galaxy's distance and speed. Exploded stars shine with the same brightness when at their strongest, so as with this row of candles, you can tell their distance by their brightness and size.

No one knows for sure how big the Universe is. Scientists can only measure the size of the Universe they can see. This "observable Universe" is around 93 billion light-years across, but it is getting larger all the time. The edge of the Universe is expanding the fastest, at what is believed to be faster than the speed of light! Every galaxy in the Universe is moving away from every other galaxy.

HANDS-ON SCIENCE

Make a Balloon Universe

You will need: a round balloon, tape measure, felt pens, clothespin

Blow up the balloon halfway. Close the end tightly with the clothespin so the air doesn't come out. This is the Universe. Draw three galaxies on the balloon using the pens. Put an A, B, or C in the middle of each galaxy. Using the tape measure, measure the distance between each galaxy and write your results down. Then blow up the balloon some more and measure the distances again. Did all the galaxies get further away from each other?

Could Two Galaxies Ever Collide?

Galaxies often collide with each other. Usually, the stars within each galaxy are so far apart that they move past each other quite safely. Any gas clouds and dust interact to form new stars. Gravity can pull the galaxies into new shapes. Two spiral galaxies could form a new elliptical galaxy.

The Universe is expanding and most galaxies are moving farther apart, but collisions between galaxies close to each other still happen. The galaxies are drawn to each other by the gravity of the dark matter surrounding them. These collisions between galaxies were more common in the past when the Universe was smaller.

Will the Milky Way Ever Crash into Another Galaxy?

Space scientists have predicted that the enormous Andromeda Galaxy will collide with the Milky Way in around four billion years from now. Andromeda is falling toward the Milky Way due to the pull of gravity between them and the dark matter that surrounds them. Andromeda is racing toward the Milky Way at around 250,000 miles (400,000 km) per hour. In around six billion years the two galaxies will merge to become a single galaxy. The Triangulum Galaxy will join in the collision and may well merge with the two galaxies also!

FACT FILE

1. Present day

Milky Way

Andromeda

2. 2 billion years from now, Andromeda is closer

3. 3.75 billion years from now

4. 3.85 billion years from now, sky ablaze with new stars

5. 3.9 billion years from now, more stars

6. The galaxies stretch and warp

7. The cores of the galaxies glow

8. They both merge into one galaxy

How Can We See Galaxies Far Away?

The Hubble Space Telescope (HST) gives us some fantastic images of space. The 11-ton telescope was placed into orbit around Earth by the Space Shuttle in April 1990. It circles our planet every 96 minutes recording images.

Hubble has sent back information and detailed images of all types of objects in the sky! The HST is named after Edwin Hubble, one of the great modern astronomers. Light collected by its main mirror is reflected onto a smaller mirror and then sent to the instruments. Data is then sent to Earth by **satellite**. The HST is powered by solar panels. It can be serviced and repaired in space by astronauts.

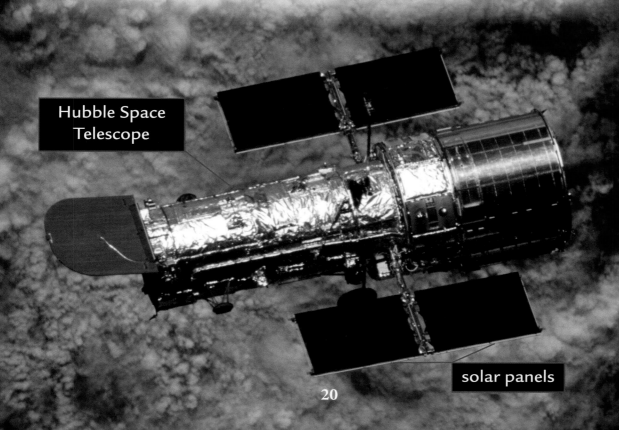

Hubble Space Telescope

solar panels

The HST takes hundreds of small images which are woven together. The final images are often a stepped shape. This is because one of its four cameras takes a closeup view. When scientists match it to the others, it creates a stepped image.

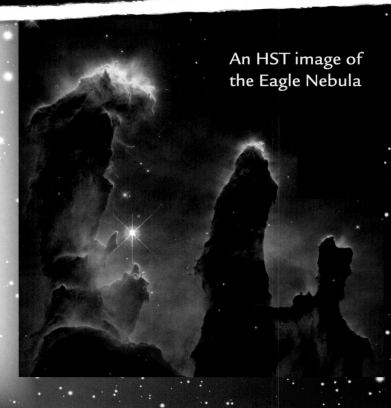

An HST image of the Eagle Nebula

HANDS-ON SCIENCE

Could You Work for the Hubble Team?

You will need: paper, pens, tape, a big picture cut from a magazine to trace

Choose a magazine picture to trace that is not too complicated to draw. Tape your picture to a window so the light shines through it. Take 4 or 5 much smaller pieces of paper. Hold one sheet of paper up to part of the magazine picture and trace that area. Get another sheet and try to trace where you left off. Do this with all the sheets of paper so you have a jigsaw of pieces. Now try to tape the pictures together so they look complete. You may have to overlap some bits of paper, just like the Hubble scientists do. Can you get it all to fit?

What Is a Black Hole?

When a massive star runs out of fuel it can no longer support its own weight. The pressure from the star's layers of gas press down on itself, forcing the star to get smaller and smaller. As the star condenses its gravity increases. It becomes a black hole. A black hole's gravitational pull is so strong that anything, including light, gets pulled into it!

FACT FILE

Two Types of Black Holes

There are two types of black holes, stellar-mass black holes and supermassive black holes. A stellar-mass black hole is made when a gigantic star explodes at the end of its life. Astronomers call this explosion a supernova. The material left over collapses in on itself to become a stellar-mass black hole.

When a stellar-mass black hole pulls in large amounts of space debris it becomes a supermassive black hole. There is a supermassive black hole in the center of the Milky Way, and other galaxies.

HANDS-ON SCIENCE

Understanding How a Black Hole Is Made

You will need: a balloon, some aluminum foil, a pin

First make your star. Blow up the balloon and tie it. Wrap the balloon in several layers of aluminum foil. The layers of foil represent the different gas layers of the star. The balloon inside represents the hot burning core of the star. The pressure from the core pushing outwards keeps the star from collapsing. If you try and press the foil star, it will not collapse. When a star reaches the end of its life, it runs out of fuel in the core. Prick the balloon with the pin. Now try to push the star. This time, you can squash the foil into a small ball. You've made a black hole! The mass of the small ball is the same as that of the big model star, but their sizes are very different.

an artist's impression of a black hole

If you can't see black holes, how do we know they are there? Scientists watch how other objects in space behave. If they are pulled off their orbit, that is probably due to the pull of a black hole's gravity. A black hole is similar to a vacuum cleaner, pulling any matter toward it.

Could We Travel Through Wormholes?

Space scientists have been looking at ways to travel quickly from one place to another in space. Some scientists believe wormholes may be the answer. Wormholes only exist in **theory**. That means no one knows for sure if they exist, but it is possible that they could. They could link galaxies by creating a direct path between them on a curved Universe.

wormhole shortcut

long journey

Some scientists believe wormholes could act like a time machine! How? Because you would both take a shortcut, and travel very fast. If you can travel at or faster than the speed of light then time runs more slowly. If you take a clock on a fast jet or spacecraft it will show an earlier time when you land than an identical clock on Earth. Even a plane ride means you travel into the future, just not very far!

How Would a Wormhole Work?

Wormholes, if they exist, would act as a kind of shortcut from one part of the Universe to another. A wormhole is a passageway that connects a black hole to a white hole. The white hole comes out at another part of the Universe. Wormholes got their name when scientist John Wheeler said the shortcuts were like holes that worms make through apples. An ant crawling from one side of the apple to the other can either walk the long way around its curved surface, or take a shortcut through the worm's tunnel!

black hole

white hole

FACT FILE

I f wormholes don't exist, could we travel to another galaxy any other way, or would it be too far? Our nearest large spiral galaxy is Andromeda. It is over two million light-years away. At the moment traveling this distance is impossible, but that doesn't mean it will always be impossible in the future.

The Problems

- The distances are so far that we currently do not have a way of powering a spacecraft to move fast enough.

- At present scientists do not believe we could travel faster than the speed of light. If this is true, then traveling to other galaxies in a lifetime would be impossible as it would take too long.

- As the galaxies are moving all the time, it would also be very difficult to land on our target star or planet.

- Even if we could discover a way to travel faster than the speed of light, any communications back to our home planet would still take millions of years to be heard!

- We would also have to design a spacecraft that could last thousands, possibly millions of years.

How Might We Travel to Other Galaxies in the Future?

There are a few ideas that just might work one day. No one is sure if any of these ideas are possible yet, but we didn't think we could get a man to the Moon and we did!

- Perhaps we could travel to other galaxies in stages, stopping at staging-post planets in our galaxy on the way.

- Some people think we may be able to hitch a ride on a star and propel it to another galaxy!

- Very rare high-speed stars have been found that travel fast enough to leave our galaxy. If we could get a spacecraft into one's orbit, perhaps it could leave our galaxy.

- People are looking at building a spacecraft that can travel faster than the speed of light by **distorting** or **warping** the space around it.

FACT FILE

an artist's impression of spacecraft design in the future

Galaxy Quiz

Are you a galaxy genius? Test your skills with this quiz and see if you know your black holes from your wormholes!

1. What is a galaxy?
   a) a group of stars, gas, and dust held together by gravity
   b) a large star
   c) a large area of empty space

2. What was the Big Bang?
   a) a spacecraft's engine noise
   b) a large spacecraft
   c) a massive explosion that created the Universe

3. What is our galaxy called?
   a) Andromeda
   b) the Milky Way
   c) Triangulum

4. What shape galaxy is the Milky Way?
   a) spiral
   b) ellipse
   c) irregular

5. Do galaxies ever crash into each other?
   a) yes
   b) no

6. Which of these statements is true?
   a) the Sun orbits the center of the Milky Way
   b) the Sun orbits Earth
   c) the Sun orbits the Moon

7. What is the Local Group?
   a) all the stars in our galaxy
   b) a group of galaxies which includes the Milky Way

8. Which of these statements is true?
   a) the Universe is expanding
   b) the Universe is getting smaller
   c) the Universe is staying the same size

9. How could a wormhole speed up space travel?
   a) it could make the spacecraft's fuel burn faster
   b) it could destroy a black hole
   c) it could act like a shortcut between two areas of space

10. At the moment, is it possible to travel to another galaxy?
   a) yes
   b) no

Glossary

astronomer
(uh-STRAH-nuh-mer)
A person who studies the Sun, the Moon, the planets, and the stars.

black hole (BLAK HOHL)
An invisible region believed to exist in space having a very strong gravitational field and thought to be caused by the collapse of a star.

core (KOR)
The center or innermost part of an object in space such as the center of Earth or of the Sun.

diameter (dy-A-meh-ter)
The measurement across the center of a round object.

distorting (dih-STOR-ting)
Twisting out of a natural, normal, or original shape or condition.

dwarf galaxies
(DWARF GA-lik-seez)
Small galaxies composed of up to several billion stars.

ellipses (ih-LIP-seez)
Oval shapes.

gravity (GRA-vih-tee)
The force that causes objects to move toward each other. The more mass an object has, the more gravity it has.

helium (HEE-lee-um)
A light, colorless gas.

hydrogen (HY-dreh-jen)
A colorless gas that burns easily and weighs less than any other known element.

irregular (ir-REH-gyuh-lur)
Having one or more like parts unequal in size, form, or the way they are arranged.

mass (MAS)
The amount of matter in something.

orbit (OR-bit)
A circular path.

satellite (SA-tih-lyt)
A machine or spacecraft in space that circles Earth.

spirals (SPY-rulz)
Shapes that wind or circle around a center and gradually get closer to or farther away from it.

telescope (TEH-leh-skohp)
An instrument used to make distant objects appear closer and larger.

theory (THEE-ree)
An idea or group of ideas that tries to explain something.

Universe (YOO-nih-vers)
The whole of all matter, energy, planets, galaxies, and space.

warping (WOR-ping)
Turning or twisting out of shape.

Further Information

Books

Gifford, Clive. *Stars, Galaxies, and the Milky Way*. London, UK: Wayland, 2015.

Trammel, Howard K. *Galaxies* (A True Book). New York, NY: Scholastic, 2010.

Due to the changing nature of Internet links, PowerKids Press has developed an online list of websites related to the subject of this book. This site is updated regularly. Please use this link to access the list:
www.powerkidslinks.com/tgg/galaxies

Index

Answers

1. a)	4. a)	8. a)
2. c)	5. a)	9. c)
3. b)	6. a)	10. b)
	7. b)	